The Value of Money

ADDING COINS AND BILLS

PORTIA SUMMERS

Enslow Publishing
101 W. 23rd Street
Suite 240
New York, NY 10011
USA

enslow.com

WORDS TO KNOW

add—To count and make a total number.

bill—Paper money.

currency—The kind of money a country uses.

decimal—A period that represents a separation between a full number and a fraction of it.

dollar—The American currency.

face—The front of a coin or bill.

value—The worth of something.

whole number—A number that is complete and has no decimals.

CONTENTS

Words to Know...2

A Quick Look at Money 4

Coins Plus Coins 5

Adding Large Coins 10

When Cents Make Dollars 13

Bills Plus Bills 16

Dollars Plus Cents 20

Learn More 23

Index 24

A QUICK LOOK AT MONEY

penny	nickel	dime	quarter	half-dollar	one-dollar coin
1¢	5¢	10¢	25¢	50¢	$1

one-dollar bill
$1

five-dollar bill
$5

ten-dollar bill
$10

twenty-dollar bill
$20

COINS PLUS COINS

You have 3 nickels and 3 pennies.

How much money do you have in all?

First, find the value of the 3 nickels.

5¢ + 5¢ + 5¢ = 15¢

Then, find the value of the 3 pennies.

1¢ + 1¢ + 1¢ = 3¢

Add the value of the nickels and the value of the pennies together.

15¢ + 3¢ = 18¢

You have eighteen cents.

Now, figure out 10 nickels + 23 pennies.

Find the value of each kind of coin first. Then add.

What is the value of the nickels? Count by 5s to find the value of 10 nickels.

The value of the nickels is 50¢.

What is the value of the pennies? Each penny is worth 1¢, so 23 pennies equal 23¢.

50¢ + 23¢ = 73¢
There is 73¢ in all.

ADDING MORE COINS

How much money do you have?
2 dimes + 3 nickels + 12 pennies

Find the value of the coins, then add.

2 dimes
10¢ + 10¢ = 20¢

3 nickels
5¢ + 5¢ + 5¢ = 15¢
Each penny equals one. So 12 pennies equal 12¢.

First, add the digits in the ones place.

```
  20
  15      0 + 5 + 2 = 7
+ 12
   7
```

Then, add the digits in the tens place.

```
  20
  15      2 + 1 + 1 = 4
+ 12
  47
```

You have 47¢ in all.

Moments in Minting

This ancient Roman coin has Julius Caesar stamped on its face.
It is from 43 BCE.

SETS OF COINS

You have 1 dime and 4 pennies in your hand.
And you have 3 nickels and 2 pennies in your pocket.
How much money do you have all together?

In your hand you have:
1 dime   +   4 pennies   =   14¢.

In your pocket you have:

3 nickels + 2 pennies   = 17¢.

How much do you have?
$$\begin{array}{r} {}^{1}14 \\ + \ 17 \\ \hline 31 \end{array}$$

You have 31¢.

ADDING LARGE COINS

You have 1 quarter and 3 pennies.
You find 2 quarters, 1 dime, and 3 nickels.
How much do you have all together?

You could put all the coins together to count their value.

25¢   50¢   75¢

85¢

90¢   95¢   100¢

101¢   102¢   103¢

Or you could add the value of the two sets of coins:

　　1 quarter = 25¢
+ 3 pennies =   3¢
　　　　　　　　　28¢

　　2 quarters = 50¢
　　1 dime   = 10¢
+ 3 nickels = 15¢
　　　　　　　　　75¢

75¢   +   28¢   = 103¢

WHEN CENTS MAKE DOLLARS

You have 75¢ in one hand.
You have 35¢ in the other.
How much do you have all together?

Do you need to know what kinds of coins are in your hands? NO! Simply add the amounts.

```
   1
   75¢
+ 35¢
  ─────
  110¢
```

You started with 85¢ in your piggy bank.
You find 46¢.
Now how much money is in your piggy bank?

$$\begin{array}{r} {}^{1}85¢ \\ +\ 46¢ \\ \hline 131¢ \end{array}$$

When an amount of money is 100¢ or more, it is more than a dollar. So it is written using a dollar sign ($) and a decimal point.

100¢ = $1.00
131¢ = $1.31 (one dollar and thirty-one cents)

Dollar sign   decimal point
     $ 1   .   31

BILLS PLUS BILLS

You have 1 ten-dollar bill, 4 five-dollar bills, and 7 one-dollar bills.

How many dollars do you have in all?

$5 + $5 + $5 + $5 = $20

$10 = $10

$1 + $1 + $1 + $1 + $1 + $1 + $1 = $7

$20 + 10 + 7 = $37

You have $37.

You have $38 in your piggy bank.
You add $13.
How much do you have now?

Do you need to know the value of each bill you have?
NO! Simply add two amounts.
$38 + $13 = $51
You now have $51 in your piggy bank!

Moments in Minting

Worn-out bills are shredded and turned into roof shingles and fireplace logs.

You have $21.
Your grandfather gives you $15 for your birthday. How much money do you have in all?

Do you need to know the value of each bill? NO! Just add the amounts together.

$15
+ $21
———
$36

All together, you have $36.

DOLLARS PLUS CENTS

What is the value of 1 five-dollar bill and 2 quarters?

Remember that when something is over a dollar, you should use a decimal point to separate the dollars from the cents. So:

$5.00 + 50¢ = $5.50

You read this as "five dollars and fifty cents."

You have $11.25. You earn another $6.50. How much do you have all together?

Do you need to know the value of the bills and coins you have? NO! Add money values like whole numbers. Line up the decimal points.

$11.25
+ $6.50

$17.75

You have $17.75 all together.

You have $16.15.
You earn $13.62.
How much do you have all together?

Add each place as though it were a whole number.

```
  $16.15
+ $13.62
_____
  $29.77
```

You have $29.77 in all.

Practice adding coins and bills on your own. How much money can you find in your piggy bank? How many different ways can you add it together?

LEARN MORE

BOOKS

Furgang, Kathy. Kids *Everything Money: A Wealth of Facts, Photos, and Fun*. Washington, DC: National Geographic Children's Books, 2013.

Jenkins, Emily and Karas Brian, G. *Lemonade in Winter: A Book About Two Kids Counting Money*. New York: Swartz & Wade, 2011.

WEBSITES

Kids.gov

kids.usa.gov/money/money-facts/index.shtml

Learn about the history of money, how coins are made, and more!

H.I.P Pocket Change

www.usmint.gov/kids

Read about the history of the United States Mint, play games, and watch cartoons.

INDEX

B

bills
  adding, 16–19
  counting, 16

C

cents
  adding, 5–11,
    13–14
coins
  adding, 5–11
  counting sets of,
    9, 11

D

decimal, 15, 20
dimes, 4, 7, 9–11
dollars
  adding, 16–19
  and cents, 20–22

J

Julius Caesar, 8

N

nickels, 4–7, 9–11

P

pennies, 4–7, 9–11

Q

quarters, 4, 10–11,
  20

V

value, 5–7, 10–11,
  18, 20, 21

W

whole numbers,
  21, 22
writing money
  amounts, 15,
  20

Published in 2017 by Enslow Publishing, LLC.
101 W. 23rd Street, Suite 240, New York, NY 10011

Library of Congress Cataloging-in-Publication Data

Names: Summers, Portia.
Title: Adding coins and bills / Portia Summers.
Description: New York : Enslow Publishing, 2017 | Series: The value of
money | Includes index.
Identifiers: ISBN 9780766076938 (pbk.) | ISBN 9780766076952 (6 pack) |
ISBN 9780766076969 (library bound)
Subjects: LCSH: Counting--Juvenile literature. | Money--Juvenile
literature.
Classification: LCC HG221.5 S855 2017 | DDC 332.4--dc23

Printed in Malaysia

To Our Readers: We have done our best to make sure all website addresses
in this book were active and appropriate when we went to press. However,
the author and the publisher have no control over and assume no
liability for the material available on those websites or on any websites
they may link to. Any comments or suggestions can be sent by e-mail to
customerservice@enslow.com.

Portions of this book originally appeared in the book *I Can Add Bills and
Coins* by Rebecca Wingard-Nelson.

Photo Credits: Cover (green dollar sign background, used throughout the
book) Rachael Arnott/Shutterstock.com, Fedorov Oleksiy/Shutterstock.
com; (white dollar sign background, used throughout the book) Golden
Shrimp/Shutterstock.com; VIGE.COM/Shutterstock.com (piggy bank
with dollar sign, used throughout book); Golden Shrimp/Shutterstock.
com (green cross pattern border, used throughout book); p. 2 Africa
Studio/Shutterstock.com; p. 3 psphotograph/iStockphoto.com; p.4 penny
(used throughout the book), mattesimages/Shutterstock.com; nickel (used
throughout the book), United States Mint image; dime and quarter (used
throughout the book), B Brown/Shutterstock.com; half-dollar, Daniel D
Malone/Shutterstock.com; one-dollar coin, JordiDelgado/iStockphoto.
com; one-dollar, five-dollar and twenty-dollar bills, Anton_Ivanov/
Shutterstock.com; ten-dollar bill, Pavel Kirichenko/Shutterstock.com; p.
5 kids counting, szeyuen/iStock/Thinkstock; p. 8 (used throughout the
book) Hoberman Collection/UIG via Getty Images; piggy bank art; p. 12
Rob Lewine/Image Source/Getty Images; p. 13 IuliiaBliznetsova/iStock/
Thinkstock; p. 14 NI QIN/iStock; p. 15 PhotoObjects.net/Thinkstock.
com; p. 17 JGI/Jamie Grill/Getty Images; p. 18 romakoma/Shutterstock.
com; p. 19 Fuse/Thinkstock.com; p. 20-21 Jamie Grill/Getty Images.